DK READERS

BEGINNING
1
TO READ

Let's Play Football

Written by Patricia J. Murphy

A Dorling Kindersley Book

Today was Eric's first day
at football training.
Eric put on his football boots.
He strapped his shin guards
to his lower legs.
Then he pulled his socks over
his shin guards.

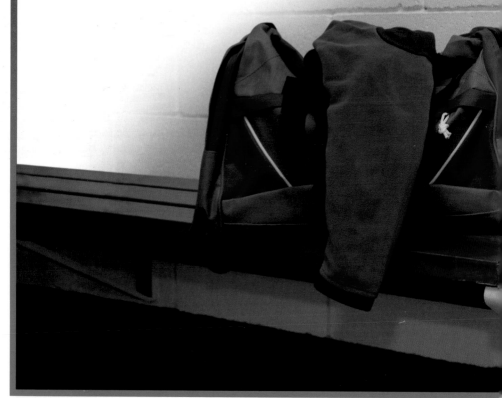

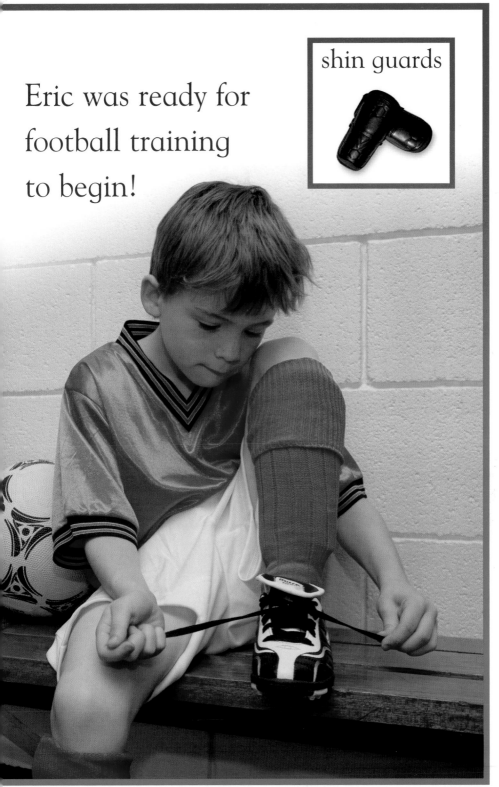

Eric was ready for football training to begin!

shin guards

"Welcome," said the coach
to the players.
"Together, you'll learn how
to play football."
He told them three rules.
"Play your best, play fair and play
without using your hands or
arms – unless you are the goalie!"

goalie

"First, we have to warm up,"
said the coach.
"This will get our muscles ready!"
Everyone did 'jumping jacks'.
They jumped with their legs and
arms apart, and then together.

Afterwards, they all jogged on the spot.

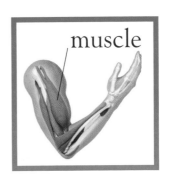

muscle

Next, the coach led the players
in stretches.

"Stretching will help to stop us
from getting hurt!" he said.

"Hold each stretch for
ten seconds."

"My muscles feel ready,"
said Eric.
"Good!" said the coach.
"Then it's time to learn some
football skills."

"Passing means kicking the ball to another player in your team," said the coach.
"It's the best way to move the ball to the goal.
You have to kick with the inside or the outside of your foot."

Eric, Beth and Henry passed
the ball to each other.
"Good passes, everyone!"
said the coach.

"In a game, you should only pass to a player who is free to take the ball."

"Let's try running with the ball," said the coach.
"This is called dribbling."
The coach dribbled around some cones.

"To dribble, you have to move the ball with the tops of your feet," said the coach. "Now, you try!"

Eric started dribbling around
the cones.
"Keep your head up," said
the coach, "so that you can see
both the ball and the pitch."
Eric tried looking up and
dribbling.
"Dribbling is hard work!" he said.

cones

"Let's shoot some goals,"
said the coach.
The players kicked the ball
at the goal one by one.
Eric tried and missed.

"Keep your eye on the ball and aim for a corner of the goal," said the coach. Eric tried again and scored!

goal

"Remember," said the coach,
"the team that scores
the most goals wins!
But it's more important
to try your best and have fun."

"Now, let's have a water break
and then play a game
of football,"
said the coach.
He split the group
into two teams.

whistle

The coach blew a whistle
to start the game.
Henry kicked the ball from
the centre of the pitch, and
passed it to Eric.

Eric dribbled the ball and
passed it to Beth.
Beth kicked the ball
into the goal.
"Super teamwork!"
said the coach.

"The score is 1-0," said
the coach, "and it's the yellow
team's turn to kick off."

The game went on.
The players passed and dribbled
the ball up and down the pitch.

The coach blew a long whistle
to end the game.
Eric's team cheered.
They had won!

Everyone shook hands.
"Good game!" said Eric
to the players in the yellow team.

The coach talked about
the game while the players
cooled down.

"Are there any questions?"
asked the coach.
"When's our next training?"
asked Eric.
"Next week," said the coach.
"Until then, remember
to practise your skills at home."

Glossary

Goal a net that players try to get the ball into

Goalie a player who tries to keep the ball out of the goal

Muscle a body part under your skin that makes you move

Shin guards pads that protect your lower legs

Whistle a loud instrument used to start and stop a game